Family's Worth of Writings

(Mostly Poems)

James Carl Stockton

DEDICATION

This book is dedicated to my wife who has put up
with me for many decades. She put up with my poetry
reading and did her best to not be too critical

Table of Contents

Introduction

Every member of my family is a writer. Some of us, like me, are working on their own books which I hope to read one day. Some of us write only for ourselves. Some of us throw everything away.

While this book primarily contains what I have written, it also contains pieces from my oldest daughter, my youngest daughter, and my late sister, Joyce. Joyce gave me her writings to keep and preserve and I felt that including those writings in the book was the best way to preserve the

My third grade teacher started me writing and told me I should keep copies of all my writing. Twice I have lost all my works and had to start all over again. From that experience I would   add the following advice. Keep more than one copy of your writings and keep them in different locations.

I hope you enjoy these feeble attempts at expression - but as I said in one of my poems:

> When you like them, then I am glad ,
> But when you don't, I am not sad ,
> To myself, I must be true,
> Because I do not write for you.

A LovedOneLost

James C. Stockton
To David Hartnett on his mother's death
(July 1972)

A loved one lost, so true, my friend,
The Lord has made it so,
All things on Earth come to an end,
All things on Earth must go.

Although you can't remember when
Such grief had hurt you so,
Try not to be too bitter, friend,
Our Lord has blessed her soul.

It isn't like a sunken ship
Where all is lost aboard,
But just a parting on the trip
To the footstool of the Lord.

Don't let her passing be your end,
Your life on Earth goes on,
For you will meet once more, my friend,
Death doesn't win for long.

      His mother was expected to die when I wrote this poem.
However, she made an unexpected recovery. I kept the poem
anyway.

A Poem A Day

James C. Stockton
(January 2005)

I try to write a poem a day,
And make it fresh and new,
Thinking of what to say,
Can be hard to do.

It's easy just to write a rhyme,
A bunch of nonsense sound,
But to write a worthy piece,
You reach for firmer ground.

I think of what I want today,
And play it in my head,
I plan exactly what to say,
And how I want it said.

Should I use a blank verse or rhyme,
Should I march to steady beat,
Or better set in random time,
Like the clop of many feet?

Sometimes I need a special mood,
Or I want a special line,
If I'm sad, I'd like to brood,
Over something in my mind.

Finally, there's one final test,
That I will make each day,
Do I put this one with the rest,
Or the three I threw away?

A Special Wish For You

To Rev. Bill From Job Skills
James C. Stockton
(Dec 1986)

Have a Happy Christmas-
And a Merry New Year, too,
May your snow be brazen white,
And your sky - a shiny blue.
May any sadness be short and brief,
Let joy and life prevail,
Don't forget His birthday wish,
The lovely Christmas tale.

May your needs all be met
and desires all be gone
And may the spirit of the day
last through the whole year long.

I cannot say very much
you have not heard before,
I hope you're not so very bored
to hear it one time more.

So in my Christmas letter
I'll send this note to you,
To let you know you're special,
Of course - I'm sure you knew!

An Acrostic Shakespearean Sonnet

James C. Stockton
(Apr 1973)

Every man should find a joy
Like I have found in you,
And I feel like a little boy,
I don't know what to do,
Nothing else affects me so,
Each day that passes by.

I want all the world to know.

Let no one wonder why!
Oh! let us show the world our love,
Virtuous love it will see ,
Each day will show the strongness of

Your love and my love for thee,
On this we say our love will last
Until the future has no past.

America 2001

(Remember 9/11)
James C. Stockton
(Sung to "America The Beautiful")

Thru flowing tears, our grieving eyes
Have seen the towers fall,
Brought down by cowards in disguise,
Who made us targets all.
America, America, God hears your mournful cry,
But only through His Saving Grace,
Will evil ever die!

The cowards stab us in the back
To force us to the ground,
But we return from each attack,
We know we're justice bound.
America, America, Our land will not be cowed,
We'll raise our freedom's banner high
And walk with heads unbowed.

The innocents whose lives were lost,
Could make us seek revenge,
When seeking justice as our cost –
Don't stoop to evil's ends!
America, America, March down the righteous road
Thru perils that we cannot see,
And dangers yet untold!

For when such evil strikes our land
We know we must not fail,
Against that evil take our stand
And let our good prevail.
America, America, The world has heard your call,
For you now hold the shining light
That gives great hope to all.

We praise our God for all to see
And bow to Him in prayer,
For when we seek His Majesty
We know He's always there.
America, America, Your sacrifice is brave,
In holding to the steadfast path
The world you will save.

An Attempt At Poetry To Mark Our Engagement Anniversary

James C. Stockton

(May 7, 1974)

It was a very lovely day,
(I was holding fear at bay),
When I knocked upon your door
Not knowing what fate had in store.

Not knowing if you'd laugh or curse
(Or even if you'd hear my verse),
I shakily went to your house
Trembling like a big, scared mouse.

And then I went and lost your ring
(Oh - that was the darndest thing),
But like a photo in a locket,
I finally found it - in my pocket!

I promised you all I could
(That I would love you as I should),
I asked if you would be my wife,
Be my love for all my life.

And then that day a year ago
You said that it would be so,
Thus we made a sacred vow,
One that's even stronger now.

Our precious love has been grown
From the seed that we have sown,
And even now, I'm proud to say,
Our love gets stronger every day.

Soon we will be man and wife
To keep our vows for all our life,
And though the years will come and go,
I pray our love will always grow.

And I pray we'll never part,
And our love - like priceless art
Becomes a wonder for all to see
And lasts for all eternity.

Be Careful What You Wish For

James C. Stockton
(January 2018)

Be careful what you wish for — you just might get it.
I have always wanted a big house
Now I have one.
But this house wasn't always this way.

I can remember a time when this house was little.
It was so little you could not even take one step without stepping
on someone or something.
Now-
I stand in the living room where even the echoes can't find their
way back.

Wait one minute...
Did I hear sounds coming from the family room?
Maybe, just maybe,
Everything I thought happened was just a nightmare that seemed
too real.

So I race down the endless hallway.
I burst through the door to the family room hoping to see, to hear.

The silence immediately grabs me by my shoulder.
And slams me down into my easy chair
with such force I cannot move.

I have no way to resist.
So I stay in my easy chair
unmoving, unfeeling, uncaring.

Be careful what you wish for-
You just might get it one day.

Beauty

Joyce Culton

(Oct 2001)

I have been thinking a lot lately about the beauty
Of the earth. We seem to take things for granted.
The more I study the Bible, the more I think about how all
the beauty came to be. What a great Creator we
have to give us such beauty to look at.
Look at all the trees and the way they change with the seasons,
Listen to the sound of a bird singing in a tree,
Watch the deer walking across the meadow,
Listen to a baby laughing as someone walks by,
Watch the way parents' eye shine
when a child takes its first steps or says its first words.
Does anyone wonder how such beauty came about?

Being Broke

James C. Stockton
(January 2005)

I'm so tired of being broke,
It isn't fun, it's not a joke,
Have to watch my every cent.
How it comes and how it's spent.

C.E.O. wants a million more,
I can't figure out what for,
Instead of demanding what he has not,
Let him live on what I've got!

Taxes rise and gas does too,
Another expense? The budget blew!
What you spend is always more,
But income isn't! And that's for sure!

Extortion is quite legal, too,
The state will do that thing to you,
Interest rates are so damned high,
Loan sharks seem the cheaper guy!

Crime is down? I think that's true,
But I can see a thing or two,
Where once it was against the law,
Now they do not care at all!

I wish I had a million bucks,
And then I think and sigh, "Oh, shucks!"
If I got a bill that great,
It would be stamped "Two weeks late."

I guess there is one good thing,
Stuck down on the bottom ring,
When I croak and done my all,
I will not have too far to fall!

Bells Will Ring

James C. Stockton
(December 2004)
(Sung to "Silent Night")

Bells will ring,
Bells will sing,
What a sight
Comes this night!
Ringing praises to Christ the king!
Beautiful the songs they sing!
Sing your songs of this night!
Sing your songs of this night!

Showing us care
We should all share,
From God Above
Comes only love,
Lets us honor this special of days,
Let us follow thy holy ways.
Sing your songs of this night!
Sing your songs of this night!

Christ's holy birth
Gives hope to the earth,
Savior , Babe,
All in One,
Humble child and Prince of Peace,
Sought by shepherds and kings from the east,
Sing your songs of this night!
Sing your songs of this night!

Ring, bells ring!
Sing, bells sing!
In our strife
Offer life,
Prince of Peace is born at last,
God forgives our sinful past,
Sing your songs of this night!
Sing your songs of this night!

Call It Love

James C. Stockton
(Sept 1973)

If -
If you have a pounding;
A feeling beyond all comprehension,
A feeling that is more wonderful than life -
Call it love.

If
If it means a longing,
A stormy desire for a special one,
A special one that you can't live without-
Call it love.

If-
If it means you are giving,
Giving your entire self, body and soul,
Trusting another with the darkest secrets of your life-
Call it love.

If -
If this fiery feeling,
Can't be lessened even with mistakes,
Can't be explained by any logic known to man,
Call it love.

Call It Love-
If it is the most wonderful emotion in the world,
If it is given freely, without demanding,
Without asking for anything in return,
If you have the truest of feelings-
Call it Love.

Christmas?

James C. Stockton

(Dec 1970)

Oh! such a lonely feeling,
I'm such a sorry sight,
I really should be happy,
I should - it's Christmas night.

But it's such a lonely Christmas
When one is far away,
The spirit of the season
Doesn't seem to want to stay.

That lovely little Christmas tree
Should make all things seem right,
But you wish that you were home,
Not here - on Christmas night.

The music and the story
Should cause me gaiety,
But they just remind me
Of those I wish to see.

Do I know what Christmas is,
Or was it message twirled?
For Christmas should be everywhere,
Anywhere in the world.

But Oh! Such a lonely feeling,
I'm such a sorry sight,
I really should be happy,
I should - It's Christmas night.

Christmas Time Again

Joyce Culton
(Dec 12, 1999)

Went to the mall what a sight,
People pushing and grabbing to
get by. Went into a shop to get
out of the way, to my dismay there
was people all over the place.

As I watch all the pushing I think to
myself what would the Lord say if
he was sitting on a self, to stay out
of the way.

This is not example Left behind. There
should be love, and hugs all around.
This would please the Lord today,
To show him we have some of his
ways. "No pushing and grabbing this
I do not like, For I asked for you to
love one another as I loved you."

Clouds

Joyce Culton
(May 1982)

Clouds are in the sky all day long, still sitting there waiting
for rain to fall. Then suddenly it begins to pour, you can
hear the thunder in the air, just enough to make you
wonder what will happen next. I looked out the window.
What a surprise see a tornado in the sky. It was not
thunder we heard. It was the trees being thrown all about
like a lot of kindling.

Computers

James C. Stockton
(Jan 1988)

Computers buzz, and belch, and roar,
They scatter papers on the floor,
Like little brats that are quite rude,
They manage to get trouble brewed.

Sometimes, we treat them just like gods,
With powers far beyond us clods,
We bow and scrape and kiss their wheels
And discard our minds like apple peels.

But, they're just a box and stupid, too,
They cannot even add to two!
One and zero is all it knows,
(Though very fast around it goes.)

Computers, they don't make mistakes,
(I guess they're right.) But then, it takes
Someone to tell them what to do,
They do not think, like me and you!

Computers are just a machine,
Not really kind, not really mean,
They don't get mad, nor do they hate,
Not even love appreciate.

Computers, now, are quite a tool,
But use them well, don't let them rule!
Let's put a sign on every mount
That says: "It's PEOPLE, NOT MACHINES, that count!"

Does God Love Me?

James C. Stockton
(Aug 2003)

What do you say to a child
Who cannot bend her knee,
Talking in a voice that's mild,
Asks, "Does God love Me?"

What do you say to one
Whose hand is a useless pad,
Asks with a shaken tongue,
"Does God think I am bad?"

When she comes a-crying,
And says; "They make fun of me!"
Then asks while deeply sighing,
"Why does God let this be?"

When those so young and pure
Brings these things to you,
When you know there is no cure,
Just what, then, can you do?

When your heart is badly breaking
From the tears inside their eyes,
How do you keep from shaking
From the pain they can't disguise?

I do not know what I can say
To ease that hurt and pain,
I dropped down on my knees to pray
As tears made my eyes rain.

I think they are a special breed
Sent straight from God above.
We can fill their greatest need
And show them our God's love.

It is us put to the test,
We have to show we hear,
How can we love all the rest
And ignore the pain right near?

When they get to heaven's gate,
They'll have an honored berth,
Love and joy will be their fate,
They've served their pain on earth.

Don't Cry For Me When I Die

James C. Stockton
(July 2003)

Don't cry for me when I die,
Don't pour your sympathetic waters on an unfeeling corpse,
Don't waste your precious emotions on a pile of organic fertilizer.
Don't cry for me when I die.

Don't cry for me when I die,
Tears will not change my eternal reward or punishment,
Sorrow won't bring life back to that rotting flesh.
Don't cry for me when I die.

Don't cry for me when I die,
Death is the friend that ends all of life's trials,
Death is merely one of life's goals
That everyone succeeds in reaching.
Don't cry for me when I die.

If you must cry when I die,
Cry for yourself,
Cry for the one who must still suffer grief
And pain and worry and hate and hunger and thirst.
Cry for the one who has a spirit
Which is still chained by the shackles of the earth.
When I die....
Cry only for yourself.

Fire

James C. Stockton
(Oct 2017)

Red and orange, burning bright,
Fire is the grandest sight,
Sometimes small, a little pea,
Sometimes bigger than a tree.

Sometimes welcome in the night
Or as a monster full of fright,
Sometimes lovely and very cool
Or even ugly and very cruel.

You never know what you see,
You never know where it be,
It can be your dearest friend
Or mark this day your final end.

Treat it well, with care, my friend,
This fearsome good and evil blend,
Or this great and useful tool
Will turn you to the greatest fool.

Freedom Has A Price

James C. Stockton

(1971)

The freedom we enjoy is in grave danger of being lost. If it is lost, it will not be lost to the communist threat, the Chinese peril, not any external real or imagined threat. If we do lose our freedom - it will be lost through our own neglect. It will be lost because not enough people feel our freedom is worth the cost.

Freedom, as they say. is not free. Freedom does have a price. RESPECT--that is the price of freedom. Respect for oneself, respect for others, mutual respect, respect for the customs and traditions of our country--ALL of these are included in the payments for our freedom

You must respect the will of the majority and the rights of the minority. No one group can, nor should be able to, dictate to all the rest. There must be compromise-give and take between the extremes. All people must work together in mutual respect. For if freedom is denied to some through disrespect-then. By the same method, it will be eventually denied to all the rest.

I am, for example, told that if you feel a low is unfair, unjust or simply bad-one need not obey it. I disagree. If all the people in the country completely ignores every single law they feel is bad-just how much freedom do you think we would have left?

A bad or unfair law should be challenged in the courts, in the congress, in the state legislatures, and by any other legal means available. But-while it is a law-it should be obeyed.

Freedom had a price. Respect it!

I won a writing contest with this piece in 1971 while I was in stationed in Taegu, Korea. The contest's theme was "freedom" and was sponsored by the local USO. I was thrilled to win first prize - a $50 US Savings Bond!

Friends

James C Stockton
Undated

I saw some friends the other day.
I did not want to go,
They had not changed in any way,
And I missed them so.

I saw them standing in a row,
Just like they were before,
We have a bond that few can know
Formed on a distant shore.

I touched their faces one by one,
And felt their touch on me,
As I felt what they had done,
The tears fell out of me.

Secrets deep within my heart,
Only they can know,
Once again before we part,
I have to tell them so.

I really should be in their spot,
And they should be in mine,
I don't know why they are not
And I was left behind.

There is a price I have to pay
To those who heard their call,
If things had gone a different way
It would be me upon the wall.

Friends

Joyce Culton
(Feb 2000)

That part of my life is closed forever.
I know I was wronged and it was not my fault.
I went on with my life.
Friends are great, friends are nice.   They share their lives with
love and care. They call you family when you're not,
they ask your opinion whether they use it or not.

They show how they care by what they do.
How can you thank them in the end?

My friends are special in every way.   They don't ask much from
me at all. I will never be able to thank them enough
for how they helped when I was down, not wanting to live.
They don't know this about me,
but I had a small breakdown before I came here.   I feel ashamed,
for what I wanted to do
was pull the trigger and end it all. The pain I felt was so great that I
felt like no one would care if I was gone.

I can sit here now and know I was wrong.
I found God nice and strong. 6
I pray to him everyday to thank Him for showing me the light
before it was too late.
I would have made the biggest mistake I could make if
I would have taken my life.

The Lord knows how I felt that day when my
life seemed to slip away.
It was then I came home and found out my
husband had found another.

God's Miracles

Joyce Culton
Undated

Everyone knows poems do not have to rhyme
Just put the words all in a line.
Roses are red, Violets are blue
Do not worry God loves you!!!
He shows us miracles all the time
The sky is blue, the sun is bright
Without these miracles we would be gloom.
So open your eyes and look around
All God's miracles can be found.

Gone For Now

Joyce Culton
(April 26, 1998)

Our Parents are gone for now, and we will miss them
with all out hearts. We
never dreamed this would happen so soon.
They were young and had a full
life. They gave us all they could and we learned how to be
independent from our Father so we could take care of ourselves
and each other when the time came. I feel a closeness with my
family more than I ever had before.
Sometimes I wish Mom and Dad could have stayed around longer,
to see us become closer than we were before they left us.

They left us for greener pastures and are at peace,
at last, after all the years of
heartache we put them through.
I am sure everyone who goes through the loss
as we did, wishes the same thing.
There will always be an emptiness that can
not be filled until we see them again.
It will be God who decides when
that will be. We have each other to gain strength from.

I received my Special Associate Degree from Las Vegas
College on the 24th of April, 1998.
If it was not for the support
I got from my mother when she was alive -
I probably would not have finished college at all.
I am thankful for my brothers Jeff,
Randy, and Patti, a close friend of the family.
I felt special and loved for the first time
since our mother died in January.
Let us all be thankful for what we have and
not think about what we don't have.

Got You Something…

To Elaine When I Found Out We Were Expecting Sara
James C. Stockton
(Nov 1980)

I got you something first before,
I did it once again,
A pretty blouse and something more
To wear - you know when!

A little pair of matching pants
That stretches when you stand,
And then - we'll, let our secret dance-
And do not show our hand!

But I'll be glad when you tell
And let the whole world know,
What is so very soon to be-
And sooner going to show!

And just because I want to brag-
Don't let me rush you on,
(Our secret's safe and in the bag
Until YOU sing OUR song!)

Why do you hesitate to say,
What is good news to hear?
Just when will be the proper day
To tell the rest - my dear?

Do you hesitate to say
'Cause you think my love is less?
My love for you grows more each day
In ways you'd never guess!

Or do you think our growing brood
Will make my love grow small?
So - would it be so ter'bly rude
To say, "I love you all!"?

Is it bad for me to see
A mother AND my wife?
Or is it bad for you to be
The best thing in my life?

Yes, I know you think I do not care
Because I rarely scream and shout,
And I know you think I do not share
Your worries and your doubt.

So let me once try to explain
In just a thought- or few-
Why even when we suffer strain
I do - what I MUST do.

First, never think I never care
When we are down and out,
But I still see so much good there
For us to cheer about!

Forever in our greatest dearth -
We have SO MUCH - you see -
Compared to others on this Earth
We're as wealthy s we can be.

Just look at all the things we own-
Look at that Christmas Tree!
Look at our blessings - some have grown
So fast it's hard to see.

A growing son and so much more-
I see around our tree,
We're lovin' rich (and money poor)
But that love means more to me.

So do not think a lack of care
Is what I have inside,
But realize that God is there-
And HE will be the guide.

And never feel I never feel
Your worry and your doubt,
But I try and plan a deal
That will work the worry out.

But I still believe that Jesus cares
And He won't let us down,
And though His wisdom I do not share,
I know he's still around.

And I believe he'll give to us,
The very things we need-
But in HIM we must always trust
And never "over-greed"!

Having The Grandkids

James C. Stockton
(November 2003)
(Sung to "Winter Wonderland")

Doorbell rings, I can hear it,
Now it sings with great spirit,
We're happy tonight,
What a delight,
Having all the grandkids at our home.

Here they come down the sidewalk,
And we love all their loud talk,
We're happy tonight,
What a delight,
Having all the grandkids at our home.

Little Abbie's playing with her bottle,
She's the apple of her daddy's eye.
Brother Ryan's running at full throttle,
Nothing but a blur as he goes by.

We're so glad they are near us,
And to us they're the dearest,
There is no greater joy,
That one can employ,
Than having all the grandkids at our house.

All the kids are eating at the table,
Their appetites have gotten rather small
You can bet as soon as they are able,
They're going to get their presents one and all

We're so glad they are near us,
And to us they're the dearest,
There is no greater joy,
That one can employ,
Than having all the grandkids at our house.

I Had a Dream

James C. Stockton
Undated

I had a dream…
Or, maybe a nightmare.
I'm not really sure-
But - If you really think about it-
A nightmare is a dream of sorts,
So i guess I had a dream.

I had a dream…
And I saw it die.

I had a dream…
And I saw it die,
And it was so sad-
So Sad -
I almost had to cry.

I had a dream...
And I saw it die,
I saw it die slowly,
A long, drawn-out death full of agony,
A needless death,
An empty death.
I watched it die...
But I also saw it when it was in its prime.
I saw parents bring treasure, their most precious treasure,
Their children, to it.
They brought their children to it, knowing it would make the
children
Stronger,
Healthier,
And when the children no longer came -
I watched it die.

I watched it die...
But I saw it when the people cared,
I saw the people feed it,
Care for it,
Joyfully give it all God could will.
I saw it, in turn, reach out,
And embrace and care for the people.
And when the people no longer seemed to care,
I watched it die.

I watched it die...
But I saw it when it was loved,
When it was loved it was important,
The most important thing in the world,
It stood for the center of the universe.
The love the people had for it grew,
The love grew - until the love could not be contained,
And the whole world basked in the beauty of its love.
And when the love seemed to fade-
I watched it die. The people did not see what was happening.
They thought it might need to be painted,
Or be cleaned,
Or be polished,
They thought the light was off-color.
They thought it showed - only a sign of age.
But they did not see the truth,
But I saw it dying....

I saw it dying….
Some people finally realized something was wrong,
"It's the young people's fault"
One old person said,
"They don't care anymore about it."
"It's the old person's fault."
One young person said,
"They won't let us do anything and they won't change."
"It's all the leader's fault."
Others of the people agreed,
"He ought to be doing more"…
So they pointed fingers at each other.
And up,
And down,
But still they were blind to the truth.

But I saw it dying....I saw it dying...
But the people still did not seem to notice.
They began to ignore-
And Rationalize-
They said
"It's not useful anymore - too old-fashioned."
They felt someone ought to do something-
Later,
The people not longer enjoyed it.
The people no longer did things because they wanted to,
But because they had to.
Things were done-
Only because they had always done them that way.
But even though everyone saw the problems-
They still did not see the truth.
But I saw it dying.

I saw it dying...
Finally,
The people saw it too,
They all asked each other,
"What can we do now?"
But-
There was no one left to keep it going
(Or simply too few to keep it alive.)
It was too late to rekindle the love.
The joy,
The expectation.
All those feelings they had taken for granted so long.
The few people left knew it was dying,
So did I,
Because I saw it dying, too.
Now I am afraid...
I am afraid because I never knew that churches could die,
I thought churches lived forever.
I thought the church would be -
It would be long after I am gone and forgotten.
And now I know it may not be.
So now -
I am afraid.

Now I am afraid...
I see no little children coming to the church,
Not for sunday school,
Not for church,
Not for anything.
And I ask,
"Is the love and the feeling for the church being passed on at all?"
And I must ask,
"Is this church dying, too?"
I don't want to know the answer,
Because -
Now I am afraid...

Now I am afraid...
I listen to the people gathered together.
I see so little joy - and I wonder,
"Is this a funeral for a church?
Are we mourning the passing of last week-
Or lamenting the start of a new week?
Where is the bounce of happiness -
The jump and the vigor that marks
The renewal of the spirit?"
I don't know the answers.

And now I am afraid..I am afraid…
But I hope it's only a bad dream,
I hope it was only imagination that has made me see these things.
I hope it was only my mind playing tricks-
When I saw all the same things in the church,
Our church,
As I saw in the one that died.
Maybe I'll eventually wake up,
And when I wake up,
All those bad thoughts will be forgotten.
But -
I look around and I see what I see,
And because of what I see, I wonder,
And I wonder some more…
Then I am afraid…

I Am Only One Person

James C. Stockton

(July 1995)

I watched the news the other night.
I saw how a woman got raped,
Some children were murdered,
I got so disgusted;
But what can I do about it? After all, I am only one person.

I see our politicians,
Many are after dishonest favors,
Caring only about the money they received,
I get so discouraged;
But what can I do when I am only one person?

I see greedy, unscrupulous people
Steal and defraud people,
Sometimes openly, while invoking the name of God
I get very disheartened;
But what can I do? After all, I am only one person.

So, in frustration, one day I decided to try something different.
I decided to pray directly to our Father.
I called, "My Father, why do you allow such evil?
You and all your angels could set it right in an instant!
But I am only one person!"

Then, when I least expected it,
A little voice spoke to me.
It was shocking to hear almost a sob,
I was so surprised to hear our Father
Speaking with tears in His voice,
Speaking to me - who is only one person.

"How dare you lament "I am only one person".
Do you not read the Bible you carry?
Are you not aware of the weapons at your disposal?
Just think where you would be today
If my only son would have said,
"But, Father, I am only one person.   "

I Love You

James C. Stockton
(Feb 1972)

Oh Elaine-
I say the words "I love you",
Yet;
It seems so degrading-
Feelings with such exclusive,
Overwhelming connotations-
Have to be evicted from their excelled height
And be expressed in vulgar tongue
By the words-
"I Love You."

And yet-
I have searched through the archives of the ancients
And the mysterious temples of the far east;
I have seen the miracles of Europe,
The wonders of America,
And even the high mountains of Nepal.
Nothing I have found in the world,
Nothing I have seen in the world
can express or show my emotions
More closely than that simple phrase
"I Love You."

I Think I'm Going To Write Me A Poem

James C. Stockton
(October 2003)

I think I am going to write me a poem.
I wonder what it should be?
Should it be full of our doom
Or take it hilariously?

Should it be about something new
Or should I dwell on the old?
Should it be about what we do
Or something we should em-bold?

Should I try to make it rhyme
Or should I use blank verse today?
I wonder if I would write a line,
Just what do I want to say?

It is important to make the choice,
It has to come from the heart.
You have to give the poem the right voice
For the thoughts you wish to impart.

Now I am ready to write me a poem,
I know what it's going to be,
Just a few thoughts before I go home
On what a good poem means to me.

I Want To Give My Love

James C. Stockton
(January 1973)

I want to give my love to you
(And I know you love me, too.)
Oh, the things that could be
If I could have you next to me!

I can see you through the glass,
Yet we can't touch as I go past,
To see you thus, burns in my heart,
To be so close, yet leagues apart.

As I see you setting there,
I long to stroke your lovely hair,
I wonder, as I'm watching you,
I wonder, can you see me, too?

The pain I feel makes my eyes cry,
But my love will never die,
I swear to you when all is done,
The two of us will just be one.

Someday, I will be next to you,
Someday, You'll know what love can do,
Someday, The pain will all be gone,
Someday, we'll sing the lovers' song!

Till then, my pain will never go,
Till then, I'll keep you in my soul,
Till then, to you, I'm always true,
Till then, remember, I love you.

I Wish I Could Promise

James C. Stockton
Dedicated to Elaine On Our Wedding Day
(June 1974)

I wish I could promise
That our springtime will last forever;
That our happiness will be eternal
And never lose its youthful vitality;
That sorrow will never appear
And loneliness has been forever banned;
But I can't.

I cannot promise eternal springtime
Because the world has four seasons,
And like the world
People find they also have four seasons-
For after the springtime of romance and the summer of learning
There always follows
The fall of reality and winter of hardship;
Four seasons in an eternal cycle
Repeating again and again one after the other.

I cannot promise continuous everlasting happiness
Because life - like people - is never perfect;
For the gladness of learning, there is the irritation of forgetting,
For the joy of life - the sorrow of death,
Thus life is only one event after another-
Some good - some bad - some simply indifferent,
And we must realize that for every feeling,
Every emotion,
At some time and in some place;
The opposite feeling will be felt.
I cannot promise loneliness is gone forever,
For it is not true.

There will be times of wonderful fulfillment
and also times of great longing.
There will be times of despair
When it seems no one cares,
And times when you know you are
The star of the world.

No, I can't promise a dreamland or utopia.
But-
I do make one promise-
I make one single, simple everlasting vow.

I promise you love.

Love;
That which halves sorrows and doubles joys,
That which brings emotion to fulfillment
And makes loneliness seem even worse.

Love;
That which has blossomed in romance,
That will grow binding in learning;
Be tempered like steel in reality,
And be tested in hardship.

This is my only promise-
I can make no other
And I shall keep my divine promise
To the best I am able.

I promise you Love.

I'm Dreaming Of A Green Christmas

James C. Stockton

(November 2002)

(Sung to "I'm Dreaming of a White Christmas")

I'm dreaming of a green Christmas,
Without a snowflake in my sight,
Where the birds are singing
And frogs are slinging
Their songs throughout the Dixie night.

I'm dreaming of a green Christmas,
With every picture that I see,
Where the water whistles
Through bayou thistles
And flows gently to the sea.

Chorus:
I'm dreaming of a green Christmas,
Whenever I go to my bed,
May I go someday back to my home –
And have that green, green Christmas in my head.

If Only Memories

Sara Skelton

Everyone is spoiled by someone. Someone who treats them better than other. It may be a boyfriend or a girlfriend, your mom or dad, or even a grandparent.

Growing up, I thought I had it really bad. Mom favored my older brother, Eric. Dad favored my little sister, Ellen. Where did that leave me? Fortunately, I had a kind, caring grandma and grandpa to love and protect me.

My Grandma and Grandpa were always there for me. I could tell them something was wrong with me or when no one else had time to listen. They made time not just for me but my whole family. They never forget a birthday or holiday. What great grandparents!

I took all the little things they did for granted. You don't know what you have until you don't have it anymore.

Everything changed the summer of 1990. I remember playing in the yard that dreadful day. Grandma ran out yelling, "Get some clothes and hurry!" I ran into the house not realizing what was going on. After much confusion, we jumped into the neighbor's car and Pete drove us to the hospital in Jefferson City. I kept thinking, what is going on? We finally arrived and Grandma told me to sit in the waiting room and wait for her there. About two hours later Grandma came out crying. I hurried over to her side and asked what was wrong. She said," Your Grandpa is dying of cancer and he has Alzheimer's." I was in shock.

Grandpa stayed in the hospital for about two years.

Even though Grandpa's death was expected it didn't make the situation any easier. My dad and mom came to Vienna for the visitation and funeral. Grandma felt so bad and I didn't know what to think. My first funeral, first person to die close to me. What was I supposed to think? Well, I finally got the motivation to pick up my life and move on.

The situation did bring the family closer together. Why does something bad have to happen in order for something good to happen? I also grew really close to my Grandma. I called and visited her more often.

Christmas of 1995 came along. Everyone traveled to my house this year. Everything was great. We opened our presents, just like every year. We enjoyed seeing the great big smile on Grandma's face as we opened the gifts that she gave us. Later that day, We said our goodbyes. Little did I know it would be not only the last time I saw my Grandma's big smile, but also the last time I would get those famous hugs that she gave so well.

Grandma called us one morning in January she was so excited about receiving a letter from Eric. It was great to talk to her. But just a few hours later my aunt called mom to get to the hospital as soon as possible. Mom woke me up and told me what was going on. I had to watch Ellen. I expected the worst, but I had to be strong for Ellen. Ellen didn't know what was going on.

Neither my mom nor my aunt left Grandma's bedside. After my grandpa passed away, I was sacred to even see a hospital. So, I never went and saw her. As the days passed she grew worse and I didn't have it in me to go see her.

The next day, I went to school and my friends, like always helped me take me mind off what was going on. After school I walked Ellen home and mom was standing in the kitchen. I put down my things and ran into my room. I knew what had happened. Dad hurried in after me and told me she had passed away and at the age of 64 years, 11 months, and 23 days. I cried for weeks after a time.

I still think to this day, what if I had went to see her? What if I would have treated her better?

I didn't want to see anyone or hear from anyone. I wanted to be alone. I wrote this poem to express how I felt.

Finally, I realized I had friends to talk to and there were other people who had it worse than me.

This paper is written in the memory of Wallace and Elise Whalen. My family and I will always treasure the memories we have of them.

If Only

Sara Skelton

If only, I would have went to see her but now she's gone.
If only, I would have been there.
Now I have to live with what I did.
If Only, I would have loved her more.
If only, I would have taken some tips from her.
Now, look what I did-
If only, I would have paid more attention to her.
If only, I would have not taken advantage of her.
Now, See what I did-
If only, I have seen what a great person she was.
If only, I knew what to do.
Now, It's my entire fault.
If only.

If You Want To Make A Rhyme

James C. Stockton

(January 2005)

If you want to make a rhyme,
It's an easy thing to do,
First you have to pick a time,
And count, One and Two.

A poem or rhyme is like a song,
It has to have a beat,
Miss more than a step or two,
And the thing will really squeak.

The sounds, they must end the same,
But the start of them can vary,
You play yourself an endless game,
(How many words rhyme with" Mary?")

The hardest thing's to make some sense,
But this you must always do,
Or else you sound somewhat dense,
Or a raving, ranting fool.

Each piece must be a tale complete,
From the first until the end,
Tie it up so nice and neat,
And finish what you begin!

Kids

Joyce Culton
(Jan 2000)

The kids are away for now, so why do I have this
crazy frown? They get in your hair and turn it gray.
They make up lies to get you sad. So you wish
they were gone from your sight. But - now I realize
Their departure creates a lonely heart that needs to be filled.

Jeff, Jr., is a pain no doubt, but something I
would not live without. He's not my son
that is true, but he is my nephew true and true.
He is something without a doubt that brother
did right for crying out loud.

Knowledge

James C. Stockton
(April 2018)

Greenhorns enter without a clue,
They don't know what to think of you,
Their knowledge is an empty cup,
It's up to you to fill it up.

You show them how to begin,
You put a little knowledge in,
But when you fill their cup once more,
They spill their contents on the floor.

Clean it up, you always do,
Then you try and start anew,
Once more you put some knowledge in,
And they spill it out again.

Repeating in an endless chain,
Sometimes it seems there's little gain,
Testing as they reach the door,
You find they kept a little more.

Then one day to your surprise,
You see the knowledge in their eyes,
They look at you and you at them,
Their cup is filled to the brim.

Although there's struggle and some strife,
Your work has really changed a life,
And that's what makes it worth the chore,
And makes you ready to try once more.

Life's Echo

,James C. Stockton
(November 2001)

Amidst the bustle and the roar,
We are thrust thru life's door,
Our cries are added to the din,
A world we don't comprehend.

We start a child without a dream,
We listen to the others scream,
Confined closely to the floor,
Soon learn to make our awful roar.

Soon we reach the twiddle years,
Start to learn of inner fears,
Start to hear the noise that's hid
Start to feel the world of id.

So full of self deluded dreams,
In a wink we reach the teens,
We mix our roar with those we play,
We feel that we could rule this day.

Soon there comes the primal years,
When within, we have no fears,
To the world we pay no heed
For we are of a finer breed.

But now, there is a family here,
This breed has rediscovered fear,
Now with children of our own,
We listen for the danger zone.

These children grow so very fast,
It seems that children cannot last,
Once, just helpless girls and boys,
Now add notes to all the noise.

The children's shadows soon are gone,
The silence roars without their song,
With help of seeds that we have sown
Our child has children of its own

Soon our life is almost gone,
We search the lyrics of our song,
Was our noise a joy to hear,
Or a shriek to deaf an ear?

For good or bad our life will end,
As we reach life's door again,
From world's noise we now depart
And return to where we start.

Living In The Service

James C. Stockton
(Sung to "Standing On The Promises")

Walking with the Lord
As I go through each day,
Working with his word,
To light and show the way,
Showing that I've heard what he has to say,
I am walking in the sunshine of my Lord.
Walking, working,
Listening to the words that my Lord is saying,
Serving, Loving,
I am living in the service of my Lord.

The struggle is unending
Going down the road,
It seems that I am carrying
Such a heavy load,
But my Lord is always with me-
That is why I'm bold.
I am walking in the sunshine of my Lord.
Walking, working,
Listening to the words that my Lord is saying,
Serving, Loving,
I am living in the service of my Lord.

Someday I'll be with Him
When my struggle's done,
Hand in hand forever
Lord and I as one.
Singing all the praises
To the Three-in-one,
I'll be walking in the sunshine of my Lord.
Walking, working,
Listening to the words that my Lord is saying,
Serving, Loving,
I'll be living in the service of my Lord.

Looking Back On The Sturgeon Spill

James C Stockton

(May 1979)

In January, 1979, there was a railroad derailment and chemical spill in Sturgeon. The spill was about 3 blocks from our house. The events that occurred resulted in this article that was published in the "Columbia Tribune" on May 20, 1979.

Maybe you ought to ignore this column. After all, I am unimportant hick person from an unimportant hick person from an unimportant hick town in an unimportant hick county.

The events:

Last January, we were rousted form our homes in Sturgeon because of the spill of some strange-sounding substance called orthochlorophenol or carbolic acid or whatever it is called today. The information, misinformation, truths, half-truths, "administrative errors," and seemingly outright deception have resulted in deep distrust and skepticism by most of the people in our community.

This set of emotions is so deep that if any of the principals of the spill were to say at midnight, "It is dark," most of us would go outside to see for ourselves.

As we were being evacuated last January, we were told that the chemical as frozen like so much ice. We were told further that it would not harm us, that it would not get into any water supplies and that is would not harm any livestock. A few days later we were home, thankful that the potential disaster would cause so few problems.

But then, people started to get sick and, even at times to become seriously ill. Although the cases that required medical treatment were rare, very few people were unaffected. The majority of symptoms were limited to persistent headaches, dizziness, and nausea.

People soon wanted to know what was happening - what was causing these symptoms, what were the long-range health risks and what progress was being made on the cleanup.

Through our city council, we arranged a meeting with the Environmental Protection Agency, the railroad, the state agency that gets involved in these things, an environmental cleanup group and local officials.

The meeting was stormy. People asked many questions and got almost no answers. One person felt the trains traveled much too fast in town (60 miles per hour at times) and that is was possibly as contributing factor. Why don't the trains slow down? Answer: the trains can't slow down for every hick town between St. Louis and Kansas City.

"How about the sickness?", another asked. Answer: You are sick of the chemical fumes, but not   from them. How much of the chemical does it take to harm us? yet another wanted to know. Answer: well, we really don't know - but you are all right. And so it went.

The results:

What has happened since then? The Seattle crew that was cleaning up the spill criticized the railroad and was sent back to Seattle - for totally unrelated reasons, of course. Meanwhile the chemical worked its way into some farm pondsand into a nearby creek. Cities downstream became concerned because their drinking water comes from a river the creek flows into.

The chemical may have also contaminated cattle and milk on a nearby farm. And we learned that another chemical, dioxin, was contained in the spill. A worker in to cleanup crew was discovered to have traces of these chemicals in his blood, but he wasn't told he wasn't told because of "administrative error." Some 20 other people have been tested, but i haven't heard the results.

Do the events of the last few months make me seem resentful, doubting, distrustful and angry? I think I have good reason to be. But then, what do I know? After all, I am an unimportant person from an unimportant hick town in an unimportant hick county.

My Beanie Baby Bear

James C. Stockton
(December 2001)

My newest beanie is a bear,
I got it, well, I'm not sure where,
But you can bet he's mighty cute
From his little brown feet to his tiny black snoot.

Of course, he is not my only bear,
I'll bet I've got a hundred pair!
They're thin and short, fat and tall,
Some even stand against the wall!

One is signed by Ty, himself,
Another is green just like an elf,
One has stars right on his feet,
Another, a sign sewed to his seat.

I have almost all, I love to brag,
Even some with a little flag,
Britain, Japan, and Germany, too,
Mexico, Canada, and I'm still not thru.

My beanie bears are so much fun,
I'll get many more before I'm done,
Where I'll put them I really don't know,
But I am sure somewhere they'll go.

It's a game I love to play,
To search and find some more each day,
I won't get all, despite many tries,
But seeking, I think, is half the prize.

My Friend Had a Birthday

James C. Stockton
(Dec 1989)

My friend had a birthday last year
So we had a party to celebrate,
But,
We didn't invite him.

I didn't think it was so strange.
After all, He's had so many birthdays.
I suspect He probably does not
even count them anymore.
My friend had a birthday
And we gave presents
To Everyone in the house.
Of course,
We did not give my friend any presents.
We knew He could not have opened His gifts
Even if we would have gotten Him a present.

My friend had another birthday
And we did not even sing "Happy Birthday" to Him.
As I told you before
He was not even invited to the party.

But my friend is still around
Even though I treated Him so rudely,
Perhaps He is still around
Because His other friends
Treat Him in the same rude manner.

I know my friend is still around here.
I know because one day He spoke to me.
He said, "Jim, why am I the only friend
You treat like this?"
I never before realized how badly I treated my friend,
Jesus.

My Very Favorite Present

James C. Stockton
(December 2004)

My very favorite present
Was not under the tree,
It did not have a fancy wrap
That other eyes could see,

It did not cost a single dime,
But it's priceless – as you see,
In the world there's only one
And it belongs to me!

Although it was inside the mall
You could not buy it there,
Although it is the best of all
With no one I will share!

It has a special beauty
And softness to the touch,
I love to use it every day,
I love it, oh so much!

My present does so many things,
(Some things I cannot tell)
They only you need to know,
It does them very well!

I love to keep it near me,
I sleep with it each night,
Without it, life's so lonely,
And with it, Oh so bright!

My present drives me crazy
And makes me put my hair,
I don't know what I would do
If my present was not there!

I had a dream the other night
And my present was not there,
Although it was a bad mirage,
It was more than I could bear.

Oh I love my present so,
It's the wonder of my life,
Just in case you did not know,
My present is my wife.

On A Night Near To Christmas

James C. Stockton

(Dec 1972)

On a night near to Christmas
In a land far away,
I learned the true meaning
Of a glorious day.

Such a beautiful day
That is more than it seems,
It contains all the meaning
And hope of man's dreams.

For it is not just the day
For presents to give,
But a wonderful time
For a spirit to live.

And it is not just a day
To see who is dear,
But the time and the hour
To spread joy and cheer.

And its not just the day
To give and receive,
But the very best time
To say, "I believe".

And it marks not the end
Of good times that are passed,
But merely the beginning
Of one that will last.

For such a wondrous day
Shall not pass in vain;
I will remember it always
And forget - not again.

One Night On The Underground Railroad

James C. Stockton

(Dec 2018)

Quick, hide.
Tell the young-ins not to cry.
Are those horse beats coming near?
Torture and death is ours if we fail.
So we have to keep
Running and hiding,
Hiding and running.
Can the next station be far?
You don't know how precious freedom is -
Until you don't have it.
Desperate,
Tired and Hungry,
We can't stop.
Every step puts us one step closer to freedom,
So quick, hide.
Tell the young-ins not to cry.
We may not make it,
But we have to try.

Pray For Me

James C. Stockton
(Nov 1996)

Pray for me.
I am the heavy burdened,
I am the downtrodden and disheartened,
I am the one with may needs,
Pray for me.

Pray for me.
I am the unsaved,
Or I am the saved who has forgotten the way,
I am the brother who needs to be kept,
Pray for me.

Pray for me.
I am lost
Or I am forgotten and no cares,
I am afraid,
Pray for me.

Pray for me.
I am no stranger,
I am as real as you mind
And as near as your heart.
I am you.
Pray for me!

Ring

James C. Stockton

(Dec 2017)

Ruby ring, bright as gold,
Blood stone red, very bold,
Make a setting that fits just Right,
Cooled from the mold used last night.

Has a bend, yellow on the edge,
Turns to form a perfect wedge,
Prongs around the end do creep,
To hold the stone within its keep.

Golden flowers around the side,
On the lacy moat they ride,
Flashes of sparkle grab the sight,
Even active in the darkest night.

My daughter asked me for the ring,
And to her I will proudly bring,
The product of a three month task,
A birthday present done at last.

Running

James C. Stockton
(October 2003)

Running,
I was running,
I was running fast and hard,
I was running from ......,
I don't know what I was running from,
I don't know what I was running to.
But I was running!

I was in a hurry,
In as hurry to go somewhere,
But it was only a dream,
I think.
Aren't too many of us like that?

Running,
Running and hurrying
Running and hurrying without knowing where we are going,
Running in endless cycles,

Getting nowhere.
Perhaps we ought to stop,
Only for a second.
It might not be a dream.

Sadness

James C. Stockton
(June 1972)

Who may know the sadness that dwells within a heart?
The shocks and blows of life that cause a soul to fall apart,
Can be hidden in a sign that none will ever see,
For your thoughts are as secret as my thoughts are to me.

Who can feel the sadness that dwells within a soul,
Within one's dark abyss wherein no light may glow,
The pains and hurts and sorrows inside a deep crevasse
Covered by the present and hidden in the past?

Who may know the feeling of one pained and deeply hurt
By an unconsidered deed or action strong and curt,
Or an inadvertent failure or a lack of one's success
That causes one to strive and prove that he is best?

Who may know the sadness, sorrow, hurt, and pain?
Only he who has been hurt and will be hurt again,
Only he whose sadness stains the limits of his soul,
Only he and him alone - Only he will know.

Sadness Everywhere

Joyce Culton
Undated

Today everyone's spirit is low because of the loss of a special
person, we all loved.

Don't forget what we have learned. She has gone to a much
better place.

She is with our Heavenly Father pain free. It is what lies ahead for
us when we are called home.

Think of it - no pain - always smiling that nice smile of hers.
Visiting her loved ones that were called home before she was. Her
children around her again, as hard as it is. We should be happy for
her, not sad, even though we all miss her. When I am at the
church directing the singing I think of her. If she was here now she
would day, "I love you all - don't be sad. We will see each other
again."

Santa Claus Is Coming To Town

James C. Stockton
(November 2002)
(Sung to "Santa Claus Is Coming to Town")

The awesome greed is coming to you,
There is no need but this you must do,
Santa Claus is coming to town.
The little one's hands keep reaching for more,
They're quick enough to grab the whole store,
Santa Claus is coming to town.
We teach them the greet right from the start,
After all, don't break their heart,
Santa Claus is coming to town.

"To want more toys is fine," we say,
'Cause we would not ruin this day,
Santa Claus is coming to town.
Just once, I would like to hear,
"Don't bring anything this year,"
Santa Claus is coming to town.
"Don't put anything under the tree,
Just bring love for us to see,"
Santa Claus is coming to town.

But this dream will never come true,
Guess I'll spend until I through,
Santa Claus is coming to town.
Got be rude, Got to be loud,
Get that toy before the crowd!
Santa Claus is coming to town.

Chorus:
He sees you when you're spending, go down to your last dime!
The push is never ending – you must be broke on time!
With little fat men in funny red suits,
Pointed hats and big black boots,
Santa Claus is coming to town.

Swoop And Dive

Ellen Stockton
(Oct 2000)
(Sung to "Mary Had a Little Lamb")

Magpies like to swoop and dive,
Swoop and dive,
Swoop and dive,
Magpies like to swoop and dive.
They'll swoop and dive on you!

So keep away from their nest,
From their nest,
From their nest,
Keep away from their nest
Or they'll swoop and dive on you!

Shoes

James C. Stockton
(December 2004)

Have you ever looked at shoes?
Some are new and some are used,
Some are red and some are black,
Some are cool and some lack tack.

Some are big and some are small,
Some don't have a size at all,
As you look down the street,
Different shoes fit different feet.

Be glad you have shoes to wear,
As you go from here to there,
Be glad the shoes your feed surround,
For other feet must touch bear ground.

If, in shoes, your feet have fell,
It is a sign that you've done well,
Step with joy on down the street,
For there are shoes upon your feet!

Snow

James C. Stockton
(January 2005)

Have you ever watched the snow?
Travels where the wind will blow,
Sometimes thick and sometimes thin,
Goes away and comes again.

Can be fine as desert sands,
Cannot stay where it lands,
Barely seen as it blows past,
In a hurry and running fast!

Sometimes thick as noodle soup,
When it falls, it makes a "ploop",
Doesn't hold its form the best,
Messier than all the rest.

Snow and people are much the same,
Watching each is quite a game,
Both are thick and both are thin,
Both go away and come back again.

Some people can drive you insane,
Like snow they are quite a pain,
Some snows are pretty when they are done,
Like people, can be loads of fun!

Next time that you're in a snow,
Think of people that you know,
Is this one you'd wish to meet?
Or rather, one you want to beat?

As you walk, make it a game,
"This snow is like", then people name,
Do this and before you're through,
There'll be more to snow than you ever knew!

Spring Break

James C. Stockton

(March 2018)

Tense excitement everywhere,
Anxious fog fills the air,
Makes it hard to use your head,
It's not because of dread.

Seconds slowly run the day,
Most sweep them all out of the way,
Counting each one at a time,
Thousands 'tween each hour's chime.

Each one longer than the one before,
Each minute adds ten seconds more,
Checking time once again,
It seems the day will never end.

Eons pass - but now we hear,
The final ringing bell is here,
Exploding out the nearest door,
Spring break has come to us once more.

Testing

James C. Stockton
(May 2018)

Testing one, testing two,
I am tested through and through,
Testing two, testing three,
They are always testing me.

Picking a, b, and c,
Sometimes just two or three,
Make a choice, Put it down,
Then another comes around.

I know what the devil does,
If he gets you in his paws,
He tests you when you hit his floor
And the test goes on forever more!

I had a dream in my sleep,
I prayed the Lord my soul to keep,
But when I got to heaven's door,
I got tested just once more!

Someday I might go to the stars,
Maybe Jupiter, maybe Mars,
It might be only to the sun,
Anywhere – No testing's done.

Thanks, Lord

Joyce Culton
(Feb 2002)

Lord, you died upon a cross so our sins could
be forgiven. You gave us hope when there
seems to be none, for this we are thankful.
We live by the commandments the best we
can. I hope to thank you in person. You gave
us free agency so we can make our own
choices. When we chose wrong, your
arms are open to help us through the problem.
We hope we choose the right choice next time, so we can
be together forever someday in heaven.

Thanksgiving Day

James C. Stockton
(Oct 1971)

Will you on this thanksgiving day
Give thanks for all that's come your way?
A healthy life, a breath of air,
A close-felt friend who says "I care."

Your life, your pride, your very dreams,
You should give thanks - or so it seems,
One should be glad or all his joys
From the summer sky to children's toys.

From the church you seek to the clothes you wear,
Give thanks for all that's happened there,
Give thanks in all you do and say,
For it could have been another way.

In other lands not far away
Others boast of less this day.
So mark my words and sing my chord
To thank our God and praise the Lord!

The Band

James C. Stockton
(April 2018)

Sonic currents fill the air,
Spreading sound out everywhere,
People strolling down the path,
Are greeted with a sonic bath.

Soft and soothing makes you cry,
With the baby's lullaby,
Rubbing you just like a pet,
Gives you tunes you can't forget.

Fast and stepping, bright and bold,
The march comes surging down the road,
Up and down with a trio beat,
The waltz now wants to move your feet.

So what is it they will do today?
What beauty will the band now play?
Artwork meant just for the ears,
Lasting you for all your years.

The Beach

Joyce Culton
(1982)

As I walk down the beach i see all kinds
of wood at my feet. I look down the beach
and I see a fisherman having a fight,
the fish is big and jumping around only to find
he has not won. The fisherman has a smile
on his face for this time he has won. The
fish story told at the table tonight will be told
with pride and honor because of the fight the
fish gave them.

The Birds Of The Ocean

Joyce Culton

(1982)

Birds flying and birds diving into the ocean swiftly
with ease. Trying to catch fish in their beak, over and
over they do this routine. They hope to find their dinner each
time. The sun is starting to go down. High tide is
starting to row in so now it is time for the poem to end.

The Doormat

James C. Stockton
(January 2001)

The doormat is a lowly soul,
Who does as he is bade,
He cannot pick where he will go,
But sets where he is laid.

Most people walk all over him
As if he wasn't there,
But he doesn't even notice them,
He doesn't even care.

He works flat on his back,
And does the best he can do,
Although with our feet we him attack,
He will stay until he is through.

Lying so still with his "Welcome" sign,
He guards the threshold shore,
Without one complaint or a whine,
So silent by the door.

The Caterpillar

James C. Stockton
(November 2001)

He does little more than eat all day,
He doesn't have a plan,
Yet goes along his merry way
Doing anything he can.

Do you know a caterpillar
Who takes a human form?
Who simply transcends each day,
Whose brain is never worn?

But the lowly caterpillar
Has lessons we can view,
With his metamorphic flair
He becomes a thing brand new.

People also have that flair
To change to something new,
Sometimes without a warning,
They're someone you never knew.

The caterpillar can become
A moth or a butterfly,
Of us, there may be some.
Who still can learn to fly.

So try not to forget
Of those you make you sigh,
A life change could happen yet,
Even they might learn to fly.

The Dream

James C. Stockton
(July 2014)

I had a dream last night,
This dream was so real I could not tell I was dreaming,
The dream was the scariest dream I have ever had,
But the dream was not a nightmare - there were no monsters,
I was not being chased or hunted - but it was SO real.

My mom used to tell me about dreams like this,
She would tell us something would happen,
And it always did - she really did know,
Once I asked her what she thought of this "gift"
And she said it was not a "gift" but a curse,
To know bad things are going to happen to those you care about
And not be able to do anything about it is a terrible thing.

You do not know how lucky you are,
You only have to cry one time,
But I always end up crying twice-
Once when I know it is going to happen,
And Once more when it happens.
I had never realize that before.

I was in a hospital - but it is not that simple -
It is very difficult to try and describe-
I was standing in a waiting room
And there were people there with me,
There were people there I was surprised to see,
All of us were very sad.

I do not know when this was,
I do not know how I died,
I do not know how long we were in the room,
I do not know how I knew,
I just knew.

We were sad for different reasons,
They had come to see me and I as in the hospital room next door,
I just died.
I had come to see them and tell them goodbye,
But I could not get them to listen to me
And I could not understand why.

I do not know where this was,

I was not worried about paying bills,
I was not worried about getting the car fixed,
I was not worried about getting the ceiling in the house fixed,
I was not worried about mowing the yard,
None of this stuff was on my mind,
None of this stuff was important at all.

I wanted to talk to everyone one more time,
I wanted to touch everyone one more time,
I wanted do anything for anyone one more time,
And the sadness I fell was the most overwhelming feeling of
sadness I have ever had,
Because somehow I knew,
I would never be able to do these things again.

Then I woke up,
I just laid in the bed and no one was around me,
Was I awake? I was not sure,
Was I alive? I was not sure,
Was I dreaming? I was not sure,
I took quite a while to figure out what was happening,
This morning - the sky was a little bluer and the grass was a
little bit greener,
I heard fussing in the other room - and it was wonderful music!
I made a special breakfast for everyone - and loved doing it!
I had another day to live - I had not died.

Not yet, anyway!

The Empty Box

James C. Stockton
(November 2001)

An empty box was given to me,
A valuable prize one must agree,
Not many would have put nothing in there,
A full box is not nearly as rare!

The look that you gave is very plain,
Your eyes are saying, "You must be insane,
An empty box, a valuable thing?
When hitting your head, did your ears ring?

"This box is quite valuable," I say in retort,
"You're making a mistake to sell it so short!,
What good would have been the pirate's big locks
If they did not have a big, empty box?"

"It's value cannot be ascertained by the eye
not by its weight, if you happen to try,
It's value is not in the present, you see,
It's value is what it is going to be."

The Empty Chair

James C. Stockton
(December 2004)

I was very hungry - so I made a wonderful breakfast the other day,
And I made our favorite foods, toast, oatmeal, eggs, and coffee,
But when I finished eating –
My plate was almost as full as when I started,
I tried so hard but I was not able to eat much of anything,
Because every time I would open my mouth,
I would see the empty chair.

Suddenly, I heard a noise in the living room,
I hurried in wondering if you were hurt,
But as I arrived, I foolishly realized everything was in order,
I had only imagined I had heard a noise,
There was nothing in the room but an empty chair.

I was working on the laundry when I ran into problems,
"Should I wash the grays and browns together?" I asked,
" What about these towels and these pants – will they be OK?"
Feeling quite silly
I turned and stared into the room for a few minutes,
Since I knew there could not be an answer from the empty chair.

The dog suddenly started barking at the other door,
(You know the way he barks when you came late from work.)
I quickly ran to the door, and stared out the window,
Anxiously waiting, wanting to see car lights coming up the
driveway,
You did not come –
The dog was only tangled in the legs of the empty chair.

As you know, our bed is so big and so nice and so warm,
I went to bed early and had trouble falling asleep,
But, finally, I was dreaming dreams of us,
You came to bed and when I grabbed you - your coldness woke
me,
But it was not you – there by the bed was the empty chair.

People come by and check on me from time to time,
As they leave,
They drop cliches that shatter on the floor like broken glass,
They are things they think
I would want to hear like "Life must go on."
Should I try and tell them that I don't really hear them anymore?
The only sound I can hear is the silence of the empty chair.

The Flame

Dedicated to Elaine
James C. Stockton
(Dec 11, 1972)

The flame I know is burning bright,
A marker in the darkest night,
A bit of heat in an Arctic cold,
A touch of lightness in a heavy load.

It's an elusive flame, ill defined,
As a coin of which there's but one kind,
This flame, when lit, cannot grow cold,
It's always young and never old.

It's always there when loved ones meet,
And often lacking when people greet,
It belongs to many and yet to one,
It has no weight, yet weighs a ton.

It's something all the world should have,
It cancels hate like a healing save,
It's lacking is like a signal glove,
You know the flame; the flame is love.

The Flu

James C. Stockton
(January 2002)

My fever is a little high,
My stomach makes me want to cry,
Not again – it must be true,
I think that I have caught the flu!

To be in such misery,
Is not a thing I like to see,
Sometimes I feel like I could die,
Instead, I sit, and moan, and sigh.

The ones nearby, they hate this, too,
Because they know before it's through,
As if my burden were not enough,
They know that they might catch this stuff.

I guess I'll live – I usually do,
Although it might take a day or two,
For better or worse (many can't agree),
I will soon be my usual me!

The Frog

James C. Stockton
(December 2001)

Hopping happily from pad to pad,
I wonder if he's ever sad,
Does he wonder where his future lies,
As he tongue-lashes the helpless flies?

As he swims through what he can see,
Does he remember his history?
Can anything ever cause him concern?
Does he have any problems he can discern?

How easy it is to envy one
Who has no worry, has only fun,
Who does not care if he is rich or poor,
Who has no stress, has no war.

We often wish to be a frog,
Kingly master of a swampy bog,
Who does not need a sense of time,
Content to swing in nature's rhyme.

But with the frog we cannot dwell,
Though in parting, we wish him well,
We dare not twaddle nor hesitate,
We must take charge of our own fate.

We must care for all, not just our own,
For we do not live on the world alone,
If with others we can not dwell,
Then all of us will live in hell.

The Gem

Dedicated to Elaine
James C. Stockton
(Jan 25, 1972)

There is a gem which I now own,
That's not been mine for long,
Each facet is a word renown,
Just like a lovely song.

Each facet has a meaning which,
Unique to all the rest,
Like the spell of some good witch
Has made this gem the best.

One facet stands for happiness
That cannot fade away,
Another stands for tenderness -
A trait so rare today.

A third one is for kindness-
For helping others near,
For always trying to do the best
To comfort when there's fear.

And still a fourth for beauty -
A brightness of the soul-
A shine that one will always see,
A polish that won't dull.

And yet there's still compassion
And sacrifice to see,
And facets of a fashion
That have no words for me.

Yet this gem is not of carbon
Nor stone that one can feel,
Though the fact defies all reason,
It's twice as hard and real.

This gem which you did freely give
To I who should not see-
We'll know as long as we shall live,
It is your love for me.

And for the gem you gave to me-
I give a gem to you-
So that you may always see
My love for you is true.

And we'll take our gems and hold them high,
Far above the ground-
So far that all the world may spy
Upon the love - we have found.

The General

James C. Stockton
(December 2001)

The General controls our daily life,
He tells us what to do,
He doesn't care if you have strife
Or even feeling blue.

He hangs there in his special way
And does not ever blink,
He watches all in every way
And never tries to think.

He stares at us both day and night
And issues his commands,
Like lemmings, we will never fight,
But accede to his demands.

So give a hail to General Light,
Who stares yellow, green, and red,
May we always bow at his sight
And do what he has said!

The Greyness

James C. Stockton
(October 2001)

A greyness has befell the land,
A parlor that most deplore,
A worry seeps out from the sand
And scrapes against the door.

It makes such an awful sound,
A yet it can't be seen,
It fouls both air and ground-
A spirit quite unclean.

The greyness permeates the soul,
And tries to make us weak.
In our heart it makes a hole
From which resolve does leak.

With one voice we must should aloud,
"Greyness will not prevail"
By standing tall and straight and proud,
We can make the greyness fail.

Cast out this demon by its name
And drive it far away,
For when we will not play its game,
We know it cannot stay.

Pass around this demon's name
So everyone can hear.
The people now know who to blame,
The demon's name is "Fear."

The Happy Meal

James C. Stockton
(December 2001)

I am as happy as I can be,
A special treat is promised to me,
If I am real good, and here is the deal,
I go to McDonald's and get me a meal!

My Happy Meal is all wrapped up in fun,
With games, and puzzles, and things to be done,
With crayons and pencils I know I am ready,
I am going three soon with my best friend, Teddy!

My bear is my friend who I love and enjoy,
Together we'll reach in and take out the toy!
If that's not enough, there is one more surprise-
I wonder what I will have with my fries?

Hamburger, cheeseburger, or nuggets for two,
Oh my dear Teddy, just what will I do?
Now help me, Teddy, I have to think,
Just what will I have in my kid-sized drink?

An adventure for two is just what we face,
I am so excited to go to that place,
So, if I'm real good, Oh, what a deal!
I go to McDonald's and get me a meal!

The Kids In My Class

James C. Stockton
(Apr 1982)

The kids in my class are special.
All kids are special-
But the kids in my class are extra-special.

The kids in my class can make you mad with anger.
They make you so mad
You debate on the best method to twist their necks
Or
Imagine lining them up against the wall
(with blindfolds)
And
Bang! Bang! Bang! Bang....
But then
Suddenly
Without the slightest hint of a warning
And at the peak of your angriest moment,
They will do some small,
Seemingly infinitesimal act,
That will make you so proud of them
That you completely forget about your anger.

The kids in my class will make you wonder why you are here.
You question your techniques, your ideals, your resolve,
Why you have wasted your time.

But-
When you are the most discouraged,
The most frustrated-
One of those kids will flash you an idea,
On a subject you taught and you were sure no one listened;
And you know you really did make a difference.

The kids in my class are extra special and they make me special.
To me-
They will always be special-
The special kids in my class.

The Leaf

James C. Stockton
(Oct 1971)

This prison cell is which I'm kept
Is as much as I can bear;
I feel as if I've been swept
Like a leaf into the air.

I fly so high throughout the land
While all things pass me by;
Oh! If I could but touch a hand-
Alas! A wind each time I try.

Why much I always be tossed about,
A leaf so hurt and dry?
But I can do no more than shout,
And my oneness makes me cry.

The leaf, they say, is such a lovely thing-
That its beauty is not denied,
They know not the sorrow that it will bring
Nor the pain that it can hide.

This prison cell is which I'm kept
Is as much as I can bear;
I feel as if I've been swept
Like a leaf into the air.

The Light

James C. Stockton
(December 2001)

In the dead valley, lightning flashed,
I came across a tunnel,
And I thought the light might be inside,
Sheltered from the elements,
But I only found the echoes of my footsteps,
I searched so hard– but I still could not find the light.

As I left the tunnel I found a country lane,
I know the light had to be near
Because I could see shadows that the light cast.
Even though I knew I should be afraid,
Knowing the light was close made me feel better.
So I searched again so very hard– but I still could not find the light.

In frustration, I ask my Lord for help,
"Help me find the Wondrous Light!
I know it is nearby because I can feel it.
Yet though I have searched so very hard– I still cannot find it".

To my surprise, a voice answered.
"You will not find the light down a road,
Or in a tunnel, or even on a country lane.
You are looking in all of the wrong places".

"The light has not moved
The light is where it is always been.
You have only forgotten it was there.
The light can be found within you,
Deep in your heart where I am.
For I am The Light,

And even when you forget about me,
I will always be with you".

The Little Baby Was Crying

James C. Stockton
(Dec 1997)

A little baby cried-
I didn't think much of it.
After all, it was unusually cold
And babies cry when it is cold.

A little baby cried-
I just kept walking on my way,
Why should I pay attention
Just because a little baby cried?

A little baby cried-
It really didn't seem that usual,
But somehow it wasn't the same,
When this little baby cried.

So, the little baby cried-
I heard many strange things were occurring,
Things so strange I had to check them out,
Things happening just because the little baby cried.

I found the little baby was crying,
Just as I thought it would be crying,
Because on cold, clear nights like this one,
Babies will always tend to cry.

Yes, That little baby was crying,
But then, I suddenly noticed things
I never expected to see
Where the little baby was crying.

Yes, indeed, the little baby was crying,
But he was not crying for himself,
It was not for any of the usual reasons
That this little baby was crying.

Oh yes, the little baby was crying,
But he was crying for me and what I am,
And he was crying for you and what you are.
That is the reason he was crying.

That little baby is still crying,
He is crying for all the people to follow in his way.
Oh, how I so dearly wish more people
Would hear this little baby crying!

The Little Lad

James C. Stockton
(November 2003)

Full of mischief, full of fight,
Little terror, big delight,
Little man growing fast,
Grab the memory – it won't last!

Little boy so full of dreams,
Who can tell what he schemes?
Little child can see no wrong,
Only good in his life's song.

Little tot, clone of his dad,
Very smart and curious lad,
Innocence one can behold.
(Too bad it changes as we get old.)

We can't forget his mother dear,
To her heart he's always near,
When he's good he's like his mother,
When he's bad (She says) like his father!

So young, so little, so full of life,
We do not know his future strife,
So full of promise, like the rest,
Only hoping for the best.

The Little Princess

James C. Stockton
(December 2003)

Little princess dress in pink,
Growing quicker than you think,
Standing up and getting bold,
(She thinks that she is 10 years old!)

Grandpa thinks she's rather swell,
Daddy would agree as well,
And even though she's young and slender,
She wraps them both around her finger!

Brother runs in quick retreat,
But now she stays right at his feet,
Right now he lets her have her way,
But that will change, we know, one day!

Pretty eyes and little nose,
Charming as a Portland Rose,
Talks allot for one her size.
Very smart! Not a surprise!

I am told I have a biased view,
(And I know that it is true),
Smart and pretty, tough and stout,
Look out world – She's coming out!

The McDonald's Anthem *

James C. Stockton
(September 2001)

I do window with great ease,
Every person try to please,
Helping all time and again,
Treating all just like a friend.

I do line which takes much skill,
Every order try to fill,
Some orders are a mystery,
I try to make just what I see.

Cooking food is quite a test,
But that's the thing that I do best,
Eggs and sausage, bacon, too,
Fish and nuggets before I'm through.

I roll burritos as I go,
They order 20 at a throw,
I make biscuits nice and hot,
They are the best that I have got.

I am the maintenance man you see.
Few here work as hard as me,
I wash the lot and windows, too,
To make the store look neat and new.

Drive-thru is my favorite chore,
Cars rush pass my open door,
Counting seconds as they go,
Rush them on, I can't be slow!

Lobby is the first you see
And I'm proud it's done by me,
Wipe the tables – mop the floor
Give you a smile at the door!

Entire Crew:
We form the crew that is the best,
Everyday put to the test,
We'll try our best to make you smile,
We'll gladly go that extra mile.

New Person:
Put those arches on my chest,
Make me one of the world's best,
Serving fries and Big Macs, too,
I'll do the best that I can do.

Notes: *Each verse is a different crew member with the last verse being accumulation of them all. It is a person being recruited. Each crew member tells what they do and then the whole team does the next one.

Finally, of course, the recruit is convinced to join. The verses are sung (using the word sing very loosely) to the Ballad of the Green Beret by Barry Sadler. My deepest apologies go to Mr. Sadler. Also, I do know that when a song tells a story – it is really a ballad and not an anthem. However, I did not like the sound of the title "McDonald's Ballad".

McDonald's had a contest for about 3 years in a row where you could submit a video of you singing a song. Tthe winner got a trip to audition for "America's Got Talent." One year I wrote this song and then submitted a video of me singing this song as an entry for the contest. I probably should not be surprised that I did not win the contest.

The Month Before Christmas

Joyce Culton
(Nov 2001)

It was a month before Christmas and all through the house.
Everyone was stirring a9nd active as a mouse.

The stockton was hung in front of the window with ease so Santa
could see them on Christmas eve.

The tree was decorated and pretty as could be.
The kittens stirred and shook the tree.
They knew they were wrong as they can be when they were
chased by the flyswatter next to the tree.

The Mystery

James C. Stockton
(January 2005)

Sh-h-h! Listen! Did you hear that?
There's a mystery in our house.
Children have always been trying to solve this mystery.
I remember when I was first asked…
"Daddy, where do babies come from?"
" Well, ah…"
I tried to find the right words to solve this mystery.

Babies are cute and lovely and wonderful and special.
It will be nice to have a little stranger in the house.
But the mystery still remains.
"Daddy, where do babies come from?"

"Well, you see…"
I find this mystery not as easy to solve as I thought it would be.
The baby will coo and giggle and make all kinds of wonderful
sounds.
It will be so soft and cuddly and give a special feeling when you
hold it.
But this mystery still stumps me.

"Daddy, where do babies come from?"
"Ah, O.K. First there is…ah"
I am going to need some help with this mystery!

Let's do what fathers tell their children to do.
And let's ask what fathers have always been asking,
(They have been asking this since the first baby was born.)
"Mother, where did your baby come from?"
I am sure she can solve the mystery!

The Other Side

James C. Stockton
(May 2018)

Whoever thought we would be
In the place we now see,
From a time when we were young
We sang our duet - a lifelong song,

So lovely then – bright and bold,
You still are – just a little old,
The color is gone from your hair,
But the beauty still is there.

Two daughters and an older son,
So many years have come and gone,
Sometimes up and sometimes down,
A miracle you're still around.

At times it seems it's been so long
Just where has our time gone?
There are times I have to say -
It seems it has been but a day.

Children first and grand-kids too,
Who knows what else before we're through,
It has been well worth the ride,
With you, as always. By my side.

I admit I have no fame,
There are no riches with my name,
The list is long for what I've not,
But very short for what I've got.

There is one thing I think you know,
That always sets my heart aglow,
Not said enough, that is really true,
Despite the years - I still love you.

Our time on earth is almost through,
I'm proud I've spent the time with you,
With your wisdom as my guide-
We march holding hands to the other side.

The OUTBACK

James C. Stockton
(December 2004)
(Sung to "Up on the housetop")

Out in the Outback we will dine,
All is luscious, all is fine,
Our little Joey has Junior Ribs,
(Even grandpa is using bibs!)

Ho Ho Ho We love to go,
Ho Ho Ho We love to go,
Out in the Outback were food is great-
We have to go, we cannot wait!

Bloomin' onions are really neat,
But Aussie Fries are what we eat,
Shrimp On The Barbie is fresh and new
But the stuff for the kids is really cool!

Ho Ho Ho We love to go,
Ho Ho Ho We love to go,
Out in the Outback were food is great-
We have to go, we cannot wait!

I wrote this song for a radio contest I entered and was thrilled to get the following e-mail a few days later.

Did you hear the good news....you were our "Caroling in the Outback" Winner this Morning! Your $45 gift certificate to Outback Steakhouse is here at our studios in Columbia (take 63 South to the AC exit...turn LEFT...take first LEFT onto Lemone Industrial Blvd....look for the Zimmer Radio Group sign...park and come on in!). You have 30 days to come pick up your gift certificate; we are open Monday through Friday, 8 a.m. to 5 p.m. (we will be closed Christmas eve, and New Year's Eve).

Thanks, James and congratulations!
Carrie and Scotty

The Prayer

James C. Stockton
(Sept 2001)
(Sung to "My Country Tis Of Thee")

My God we pray to Thee,
Us sinners that you see,
We pray as one,
You've fashioned quite a test,
For all of us you blessed,
For you, Our Lord, we'll do our best
Great God our King.

Our Lord, we pray to Thee,
Help save our liberty.
Help us be brave.
Help us to see thy will,
Thy wishes to fulfill,
We sing thy praises still-
Great God our King.

Help us to wage the fight,
Serve mercy with our might,
Keep our cause true.
Keep us within your sight,
On guard throughout the night,
Help us to do what's right-
Great God our King.

Hold off the tempter's snare,
Serve justice everywhere,
For this we pray.
Give us the faith of Paul,
Help us to hear your call,
When with you we cannot fall-
Great God our King.

I give my thanks to Thee
For all you've give to me,
Amen my Lord.
Help me to see thy will,
Thy wishes to fulfill,
I sing thy praises still-
Great God my King.

The Puzzle

James C. Stockton
(Dec 2018)

Puzzles pieces everywhere,
Puzzles picture on the chair,
Everything in disarray,
Let's see what we can do today.

Find a piece that's straight and true,
"Edges first" should be a rule,
Most have four within the box
To form a frame as each piece locks.

Find a pattern in the piles
And work upon it for a while,
Working outward like a wheel,
A bigger part you'll soon reveal.

Connect the patterns to the frame
Until a tiny few remain,
The last ones can be hard to do
And sometimes form a test for you.

Finally, you've got them all,
Every piece, both big and small.
The smile you earned can now begin
As you drop the last piece in.

The Rule

James C. Stockton
(January 2001)

Years, and Months, and Weeks, and Days,
When born we start our dying ways,
Marching constantly towards the night,
An instinctive urge we cannot fight.

For some, the trip is very curt,
From birth they do an endline spurt,
Others wither on the vine,
And take years to find the line.

Why must we die? It is not known,
There is no pattern that has been shown,
Nature's secret is not revealed,
Nevertheless, our fate is sealed.

But there are things that I have found,
When I have chance to look around,
Things like rocks, they do not die,
Neither clouds which pass us by.

Yet animals see their demise,
So do trees which seek the skies,
Such a fate awaits all the plants,
Even insects, such as ants.

Living or not, I see one rule
Which, I guess, is always true,
Tough sounding odd, it has great depth,
This is the rule: Life causes death.

The Strange Flame

Dedicated to Elaine
James C. Stockton
(Dec 8, 1972)

The strangest flame burns in my soul
That does weird things to me-
My feet - They know not where to go,
My eyes - They will not see.

My mind is full of crazy thoughts,
My logic - it has fled,
My heart is tied in sailor's knots,
My brain has left my head.

This strange new light that I have seen
I've never seen before-
Tis lovely as crystal's sheen-
Times ten thousand more.

What makes this flame that I now own
I simply cannot say,
But - like a new seed freshly sown -
Gets stronger every day.

What caused this thing to now appear?
I think that I might know-
For since the time I found one dear-
My heart's been all aglow

The Stranger

James C. Stockton
(October 2003)

The stranger sits upon the bench,
The air transmits the awful stench,
The dress is strange and rather crude,
The very sight is simply rude.

The stranger does not seem quite right,
You try to void the frightening sight,
The stranger is still sitting there-
Try to pretend you do not care!

You pray the contact will not last,
So hurry, hurry, hurry past!
For if you look you just might see
Who the stranger now will be.

The stranger goes on rushing by
As you detect an angry sigh,
You know the stranger must be late
To run at such a rapid rate!

Just who is now the stranger here?
Who is it we are to fear?
Was that a stranger? Think again,
Or did you lose an unknown friend?

The Sub

James C. Stockton
(May 1991)

The sub is but a hardy food
Who sits in every class.
Who shouts a bit a time or two
And waits for time to pass.

The sub must be an expert on
All subjects small and great.
He never knows what waits him next.
He dares to temp his fate.

He's History now and English next,
French and Spanish, too!
They either think he's very smart
Or lacks a think or two!

He doesn't know a student one
So he searches out the chart.
Since it was done in '73
Must be a work of art!

He doesn't know what they're working on
Or assignments he must give.
The faces of the ruffians glean-
It is their day to live!

The sordid note the teacher left
Say, "They know just what to do."
But if you ask what that might be,
The students say, "Huh! Who?"

The sub is such a gifted lot
That teaches with such ease.
The work that quote "would last a week."
Is finished in a breeze!

He steps into another's shoes
And then steps out again.
He's sure to be called once more
(Though never knows quite when.)

The Sub 2

James C. Stockton
(April 2018)

Bouncing down the learned hall,
You're supposed to do it all,
Flimsy papers for a guide,
How it goes you must decide.

Students filter through the door,
They drop brains on the floor,
Knowledge learned is all forgot,
No matter what, they know it not.

Talking loud with jerking head,
The noise they make can wake the dead,
No matter what you do or say,
You know it is a wasted day.

But you still will try your best,
Each new day, another test.
On bad days you cannot dwell,
You live for days where things go well.

Wandering from school to school,
You often feel as a fool,
Usually for just a day,
You try to help them anyway.

They don't know that they are gold,
(They won't know 'till they're old.)
Rough and ragged to your sight,
They are our future's only light.

So you go from day to day,
Try to urge them on their way,
If you can only reach one life,
It was well worth all the strife.

The Waves

Joyce Culton

(1982)

The rock in the ocean stands so tall when the waves
hit they split apart. It is a pretty sight to see one
of God's creations can look so sweet. They come
together again before reaching the beach so the waves still can
roll up to your feel. The water is cold the weather is
warm. The fishers lined along the beach in hope of
catching a fish - that would be neat. Now it is time to
go on the road to Uncle Al's in Klamath where he
has a resort he is saving a cabin just for me. The next
four days it will be sweet to sleep nice and long without
a phone ringing within ten feet.

These Athletes

James C. Stockton
(January 2002)

These athletes are so special,
They play with all their soul,
And all their heart,
And all their mind,
But you can only give Gold medals
To some of them,
But they all deserve one.

These athletes are so special,
They play with all their soul
Because their intent is so pure,
They play with all their heart
Because they get a chance to do what others do,
They play with all their mind
Because they are eager to show what they can do,
They all deserve Gold medals
But some will have to get Silver.

These athletes are so special,
Because they play with all their soul
We are drawn to their games,
Because they play with all their heart
We cheer for them as if every event was the Super Bowl,
Because they play with all their mind
We laugh with them at the occasional gaff,
They all deserve Gold medals
But some will only get a Bronze.

These athletes are so special,
Whether they get to bring home the Gold,
Or they have to settle for the Silver,
Or they try valiantly and get only the Bronze,
Or, even, just a ribbon for trying their best,
These special athletes,
The athletes of the Special Olympics,
Are all winners!

Thirty Years Too Late

James C. Stockton
(November 2001)

The music was so grand
That I heard the other day,
A patriotic band
Was playing, by the way.

A Flag was flying high,
It stirred inside my soul,
But I could only sigh,
Old memories took control.

I wish that I could forget
The things I've had to see;
Like concrete, in my mind they're set,
They're such a part of me.

A smell, a touch, or just a sound
Can start a memory,
Then I am standing on that ground
Were I do, I feel, and I see.

With great sadness, I remember
Those who died in history,
Some were so much better-
Why them, why not me?

There was a friend named Wayne
Who stormed thru Heaven's gate-
For him, the band was playing
Thirty years too late.

I wonder, will the music fade?
Will the flag be taken down?
What about those we have made
To walk upon that ground?

What about the ones today?
What will be their fate?
Will they also have to say,
"The band has played too late."?

Ticking Away

James C. Stockton
(Nov 1972)

We live alongside an endless stream of time -
With incomprehensible rocks,
And rapids.
We can only begin to measure its length
By the seconds
That keep ticking away.

We - like small empires and kingdoms-
Build and destroy and rebuild - again
Everything
All that we care for and enjoy each year
Which is just a small summary of the seconds
That keep ticking away.

And we go forward as if there will always be a tomorrow-
A never ending segment of time,
Always
And yet - whether we live or die
Whether we be famous or unknown.
We see only a microscope piece of that river;
And when we are dead
The hours and the days and months and years
Will go endlessly on
Powered by an infinite numbers of seconds
That keep ticking away.

To Bill

James C. Stockton

(Dec 1987)

We wanted to put your present
In a big and fancy box
But just couldn't find one
That jumps, and sings, and talks!

We wanted to make your present
An instant lottery prize,
But we couldn't find a ticket
That said "Birthday present surprise!"

We wanted to put your present
In what the French refer to as "coach"-
But the fanciest car we could find
Was a little funny brown roach!

So we had to put your present
In the dirty wind-blown sack,
(Hardly a proper and fitting way
To pay your kindness back!)

Although the wrapper's not fancy
And doesn't glitter in the eyes,
Think of it as a wonder--
Love and caring in disguise!

To The Critic

James C. Stockton
(December 2004)

You say, "It doesn't fit the forms,"
You say, "It doesn't follow norms,"
"It lacks style." That may be true,
But then, I did not write for you.

You tell me that it lacks finesse,
You tell me that it's not the best,
You're the expert – that is true,
But then, I did not write for you.

Emotions that I had to say,
I had to do in my own way,
It had to sound just right, you see,
The one that I write for is me.

When you like them, then I am glad,
But when you don't, I am not sad,
To myself, I must be true,
Because I do not write for you.

To The One I Love

To Elaine
James C. Stockton
(March 1973)

To the one I love I say,
"No tribute can befall you which will do you justice;"
For--you among all others are unique,
And you - only you-
Posses the perfect combination of personality
And beauty,
And because of this (and more) I love you.

I love you for your humor-
Which can make the most painful situation bearable;
For your kindness-
Which makes you care for others before yourself
And makes others happy just by knowing you;
For your strength-
That helps you accept and master challenging situations
Which leaves others in disarray;
For your happiness-
Which radiates out and infects others with spirits of goodwill;
For your talents-
Which are many in number and highly developed,
Because of this (and much more) I love you.

But besides all of these reasons
(And the many more I could name),
There is one thing that I love about you
That stands above the rest.
One thing is so wonderful that I cannot help but love it.

That Is You,

YOU-who is apart from the rest;
YOU-who has her own special points (both good and bad);
YOU- who doesn't pretend to be anything but yourself;
Yes-YOU-with the perfect combination of "beauty and brains" that
makes you unique;
Yes, dear, I love YOU for what you are-
Perhaps-not flawless,
Perhaps-never winning Miss Universe
(But still lovely).
I love YOU-that unique woman.
I love YOU for what you are'
YOURSELF!

Tough Your Logic Says

To Richard When We Thought His Father Was Going To Die
James C. Stockton
(1973)

Your logic says that all is done
And death, from you, has taken one
Whom you've loved and held most dear;
Logic says he's gone from here.

Logic says you should be sad,
Fate has taken what you had
And left a pain deep in your heart;
Such pain, you feel, will never part.

And Logic says that all is lost
And fate, just like a summer's frost,
Has killed all that deserve to live
And taken more the you should give.

But logic should not rule your day-
For logic is but man's way
of taking all that God has caused
And binding it to man-made laws.

For you should not be sad, but gay,
Though one you loved has gone away;
For death is nothing but a sleep,
Death may claim, but he can't keep.

And death is like a swinging door
Which opens to another floor,
Where life is real and never ends,
Where one will find some long-lost friends.

And death is like an ocean cruise,
Full of joy and lovely views
Of heaven where God himself does reign,
Of heaven where you will meet again.

So - do not be sad he's gone away,
For you will follow him one day,
When you say he reached life's end-
Eternal life will now begin.

When Anger Strikes

Joyce Culton
Undated

We all get upset when we have problems. We must remind people what the Lord said, Love one another, as I have loved you (John 15:12).

Remember when Peter as having problems with his brother, kept sinning against him, he asked the Lord how many times he should forgive and the Lord said seventy times seven. (Matthew 18:22) then in (Matthew 5:44) the Lord said a to love your enemies, bless them that curse you, do good to them that hate you, and pray for them which despitefully use you, and prosecute you.

If we would live with these three verses in mind, life would be smoother for everyone. We were put here on earth to prove we can follow the example of Jesus Christ and earn our way back to live again in heaven with our Heavenly Father.

When I Am Gone

James C. Stockton
(1999)

When I am gone and my life is through,
There is a fact I know is true,
No one will know I've been around.
A common wail, and Sad I've found.

In one year, two, or maybe ten,
My name will not be spoken again.
A wisp of smoke that does not last,
Resigned to man's forgotten past.

By now, I know it is my fate
To never be a man who's great.
To never be on top and glow,
But underneath, in depths below.

So, why then, life? It is so small.
Why bother then to live at all?
Why should we struggle, care or try?
All is gone, when once we die.

I guess I'm like a grain of sand.
Alone, I make so little land,
But with all the rest around,
We do make quite a bit of ground.

So like the beach beneath your feet,
The common sands congeal and meet;
Alone, one grain is much like me,
Together they hold against the sea.

The future is upon our back,
In our sand it makes its track,
Without us all beneath its toe,
The future has nowhere to go.

Thus, I'm content to be the sand,
On which those yet to come will stand.
Knowing all is vital, indeed,
Fulfilling, not mine, but a greater need.

Winter Weather

Joyce Culton
(Dec 12, 1999)

Winter weather is here cold everywhere. The wind is blowing
what a chill.
that will not go away. It seems like it sticks to your soul, and we
know it is not
snow. It blows through you at a great speed. It seems to bring us
to our knees.
People are standing around hoping the city bus is coming around
the corner.

Now that we are on the bus, we stop and wonder what was the
fuss. Then
we remember when the bus stops. We wish it would snow, so it
would not
be so cold.

Wonders

Joyce Culton
(1982)

As I sit and watch the ocean row in and out. I wonder what
it is all about. The ocean must be ready to go asleep, looks
like the clouds are at its feet. The ocean sounds pretty in the
sunset, now it is time for the ocean to rest. So I head back
to my car and head up the street where I live to support the
fleet.

Words

James C. Stockton

(May 1973)

(Written when I discovered all the entire collection of poems I
had written had been lost)

I guess they were nothing but words.
Words in dried-out and faded lines,
Words which have no monetary value,
Words of such little importance,
That they cannot be recalled.

These words were like the names of forgotten persons.
Persons, whose names are forgotten in history.
Persons, whose names have no monetary value.
Persons, whose names are so unimportant
That they cannot be recalled.

For who knows the names of the fearsome invaders
Who threw their burning flames into
The Ancient Library of Alexandria?
They, who themselves, created so many forgotten words.
Words as forgotten as the names of the invaders.

And what are the names of the persons
Who captured the lions for Nero's circus?
Nero's taste for raw human flesh
Caused many forgotten words to be said.
Words as forgotten as the names of the trappers.

Yet, how the world would have missed the unimportant persons.
These persons whose names have been forgotten by history,
These persons whose names have no monetary value,
These persons whose names
Cannot be recalled.

And words, like the names, are nothing but symbols for sounds,
Patches of vibrations that disperse in the air.
Patches of vibrations using and erg or two of energy.
Patches of vibrations, once sent on their way,
Cannot be recalled.
And like one lingers for the fading vibration of loosened sound
And like the world misses the names of forgotten persons,
I will miss these forgotten words.
These forgotten words which expressed all the joy and sorrow
Which I have felt in my unimportant life.
These forgotten words which were once a part of my soul.
These forgotten words which
Cannot be recalled.

You Want Me To Rap

James C. Stockton
(January 2005)

You want me to rap? I am amazed,
Somewhat confused and partially dazed.
It is something that I probably can't do,
If you listen to me, I'll explain it to you.

It isn't because I cannot make rhyme,
I do it for fun much of the time,
It isn't because I don't want to try,
But I really don't think I'm quite the right guy.

To any good work you bring what you know,
It comes from your heart and deep in your soul,
It comes from your life, what you've seen and you've done,
Because of this fact I'm not the one.

You have traveled your path one step at a time,
Sometimes it's unjust and sometimes it's unkind,
Although we both traveled to the place where we are,
The path that I traveled is different by far.

It's not that one's good and the other is bad,
Just different experiences that each of us had,
One simple rule that is not really news,
You cannot know another 'till you walked in their shoes!

Looking at one thing, both now together,
You will see one side and I'll see the other,
Rap's a way of expression, an art form that's pure,
I don't have the background, I know that for sure.

I don't even know how to start or begin,
The middle's a mystery and so is the end.
We can learn from each other, that is certainly true,
But in the end – I am me – And you are still you.

Made in the USA
Monee, IL
27 April 2022

95545580R00105